Paul Revere's RIDE

by Xavier Niz

illustrated by Brian Bascle

Consultant:

Wayne Bodle, Assistant Professor of History

Indiana University of Pennsylvania

Indiana, Pennsylvania

Capstone press

Mankato, Minnesota

Graphic Library is published by Capstone Press,
151 Good Counsel Drive, P.O. Box 669, Mankato, Minnesota 56002.
www.capstonepress.com

Printed in the United States of America

1 2 3 4 5 6 10 09 08 07 06 05

Library of Congress Cataloging-in-Publication Data
Niz, Xavier.
Paul Revere's ride / by Xavier Niz ; illustrated by Brian Bascle.
p. cm.—(Graphic library. Graphic history)
Includes bibliographical references and index.
ISBN 0-7368-4965-3 (hardcover)
1. Revere, Paul, 1735–1818—Juvenile literature. 2. Massachusetts—History—Revolution, 1775–1783—Juvenile literature. 3. Lexington, Battle of, Lexington, Mass., 1775—Juvenile literature. 4. Concord, Battle of, Concord, Mass., 1775—Juvenile literature. 5. Statesmen—Massachusetts—Biography—Juvenile literature. 6. Massachusetts—Biography—Juvenile literature. I. Bascle, Brian, ill. II. Title. III. Series.
F69.R43N59 2006
973.3'311'092—dc22 200500652

Summary: In graphic novel format, tells the story of Paul Revere's ride to Lexington in April 1775 to warn colonists of approaching British troops.

Art and Editorial Direction
Jason Knudson and Blake A. Hoena

Designers
Bob Lentz and Juliette Peters

Editor
Donald Lemke

Editor's note: Direct quotations from primary sources are indicated by a yellow background.

Direct quotations appear on the following pages:

Pages 12, 20, from *Paul Revere's Three Accounts of His Famous Ride* by Paul Revere (Boston: Massachusetts Historical Society, 1976).

Pages 14, 19, from *Paul Revere's Ride* by David Hackett Fischer (New York: Oxford University Press, 1994).

TABLE of CONTENTS

Chapter 1
The General's Plan

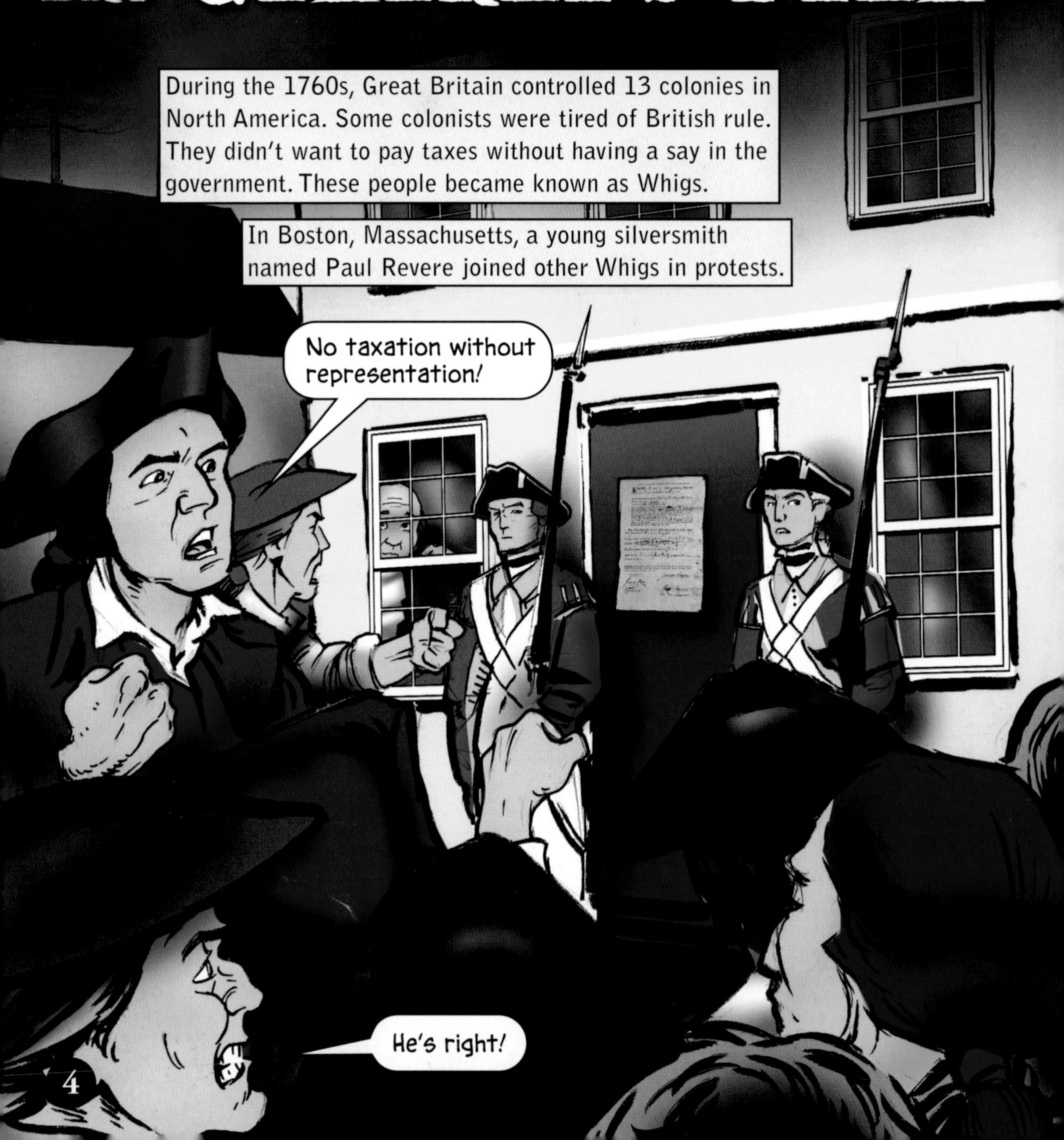
During the 1760s, Great Britain controlled 13 colonies in North America. Some colonists were tired of British rule. They didn't want to pay taxes without having a say in the government. These people became known as Whigs.
In Boston, Massachusetts, a young silversmith named Paul Revere joined other Whigs in protests.
No taxation without representation!
He's right!

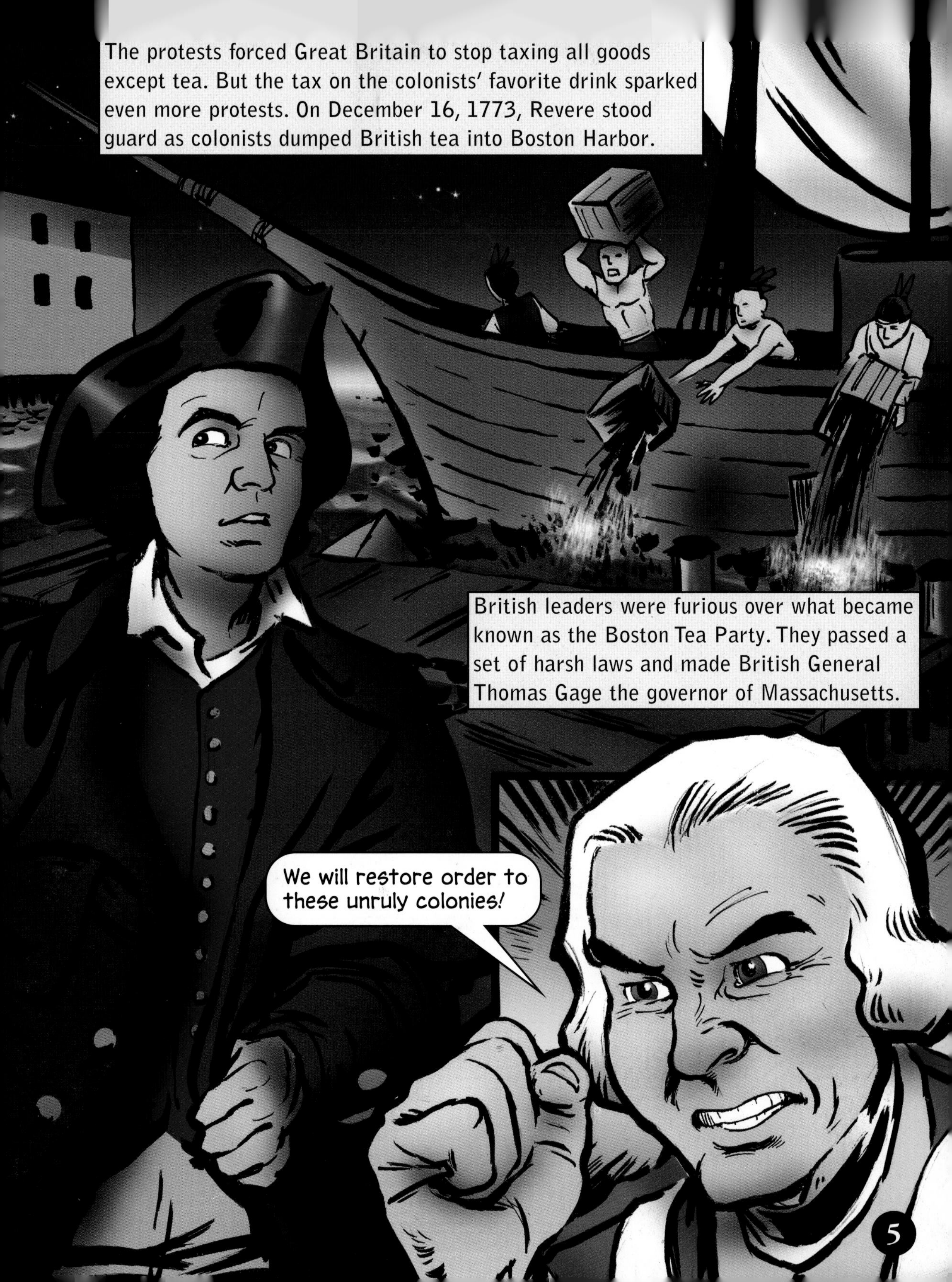

The protests forced Great Britain to stop taxing all goods except tea. But the tax on the colonists' favorite drink sparked even more protests. On December 16, 1773, Revere stood guard as colonists dumped British tea into Boston Harbor.
British leaders were furious over what became known as the Boston Tea Party. They passed a set of harsh laws and made British General Thomas Gage the governor of Massachusetts.
We will restore order to these unruly colonies!

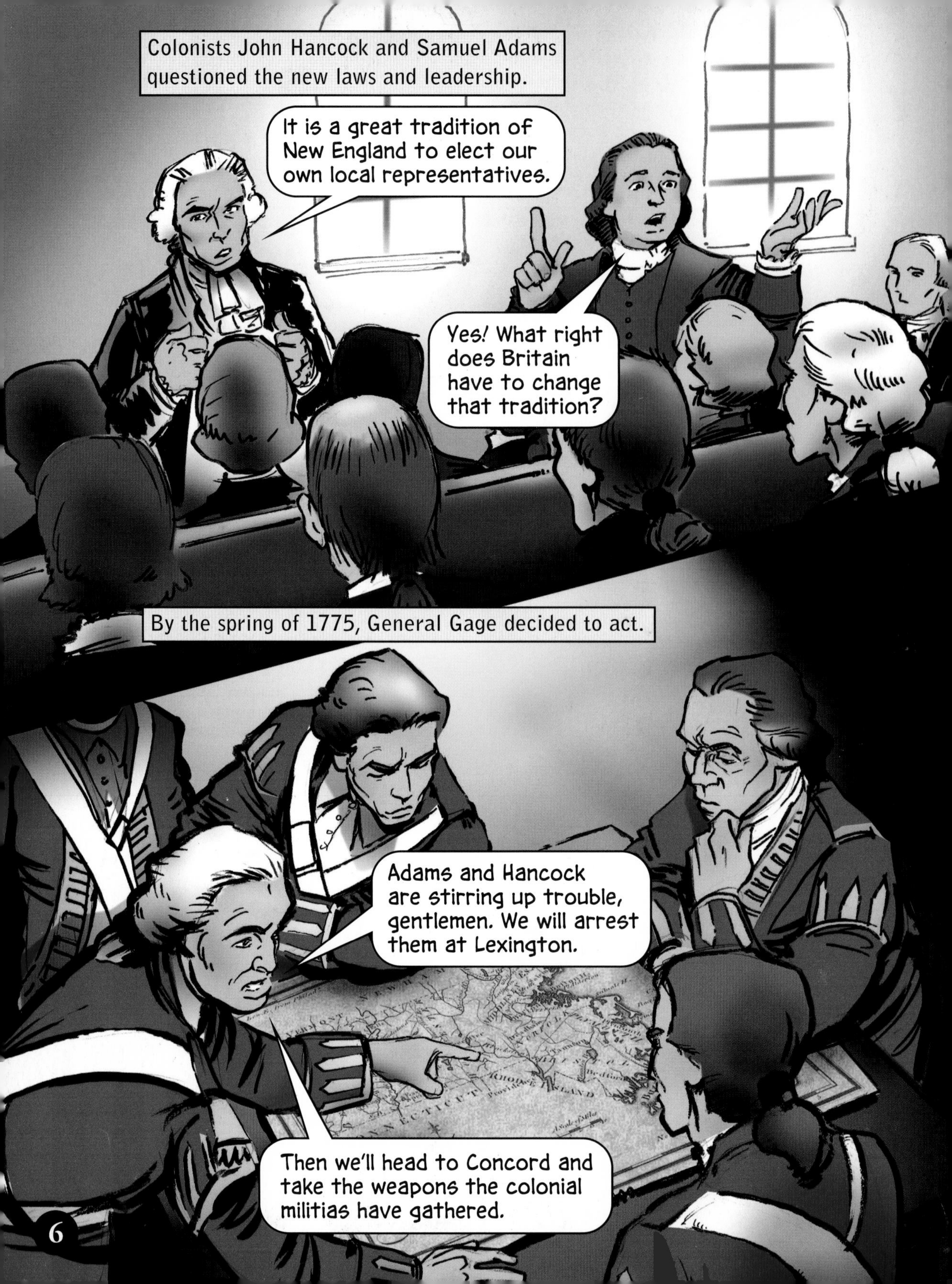
Colonists John Hancock and Samuel Adams questioned the new laws and leadership.
It is a great tradition of New England to elect our own local representatives.
Yes! What right does Britain have to change that tradition?
By the spring of 1775, General Gage decided to act.
Adams and Hancock are stirring up trouble, gentlemen. We will arrest them at Lexington.
Then we'll head to Concord and take the weapons the colonial militias have gathered.

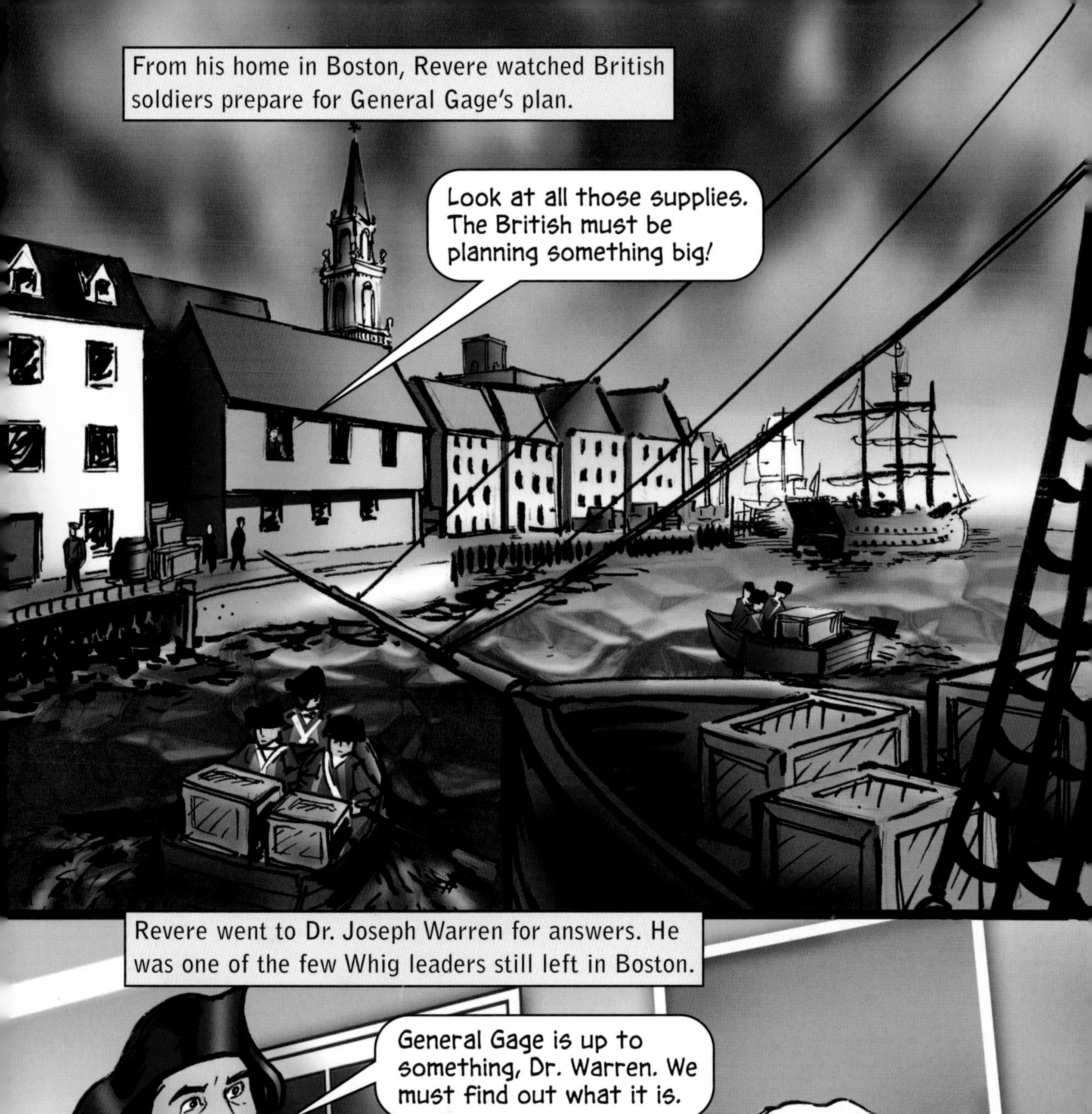
From his home in Boston, Revere watched British soldiers prepare for General Gage's plan.
Look at all those supplies. The British must be planning something big!

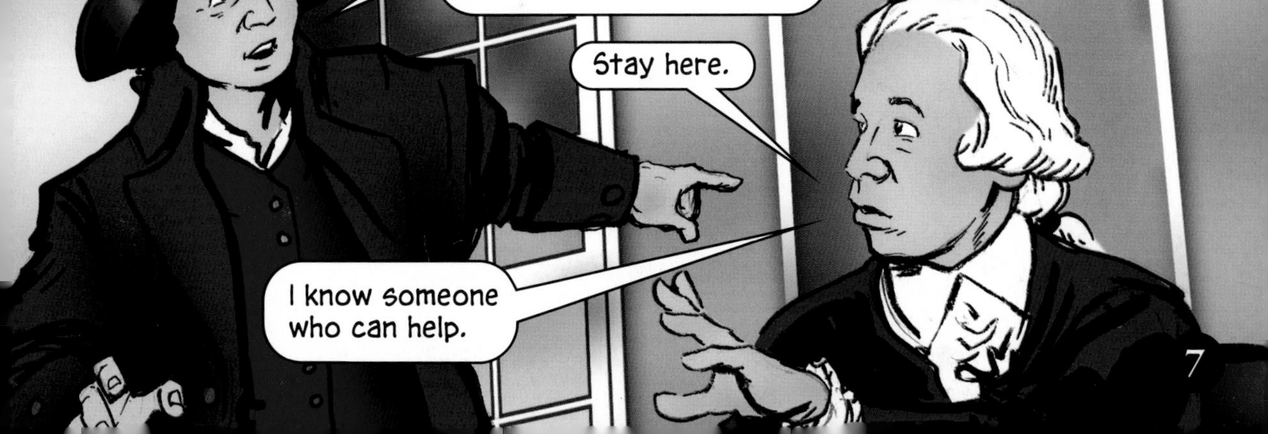
Revere went to Dr. Joseph Warren for answers. He was one of the few Whig leaders still left in Boston.
General Gage is up to something, Dr. Warren. We must find out what it is.
Stay here.
I know someone who can help.

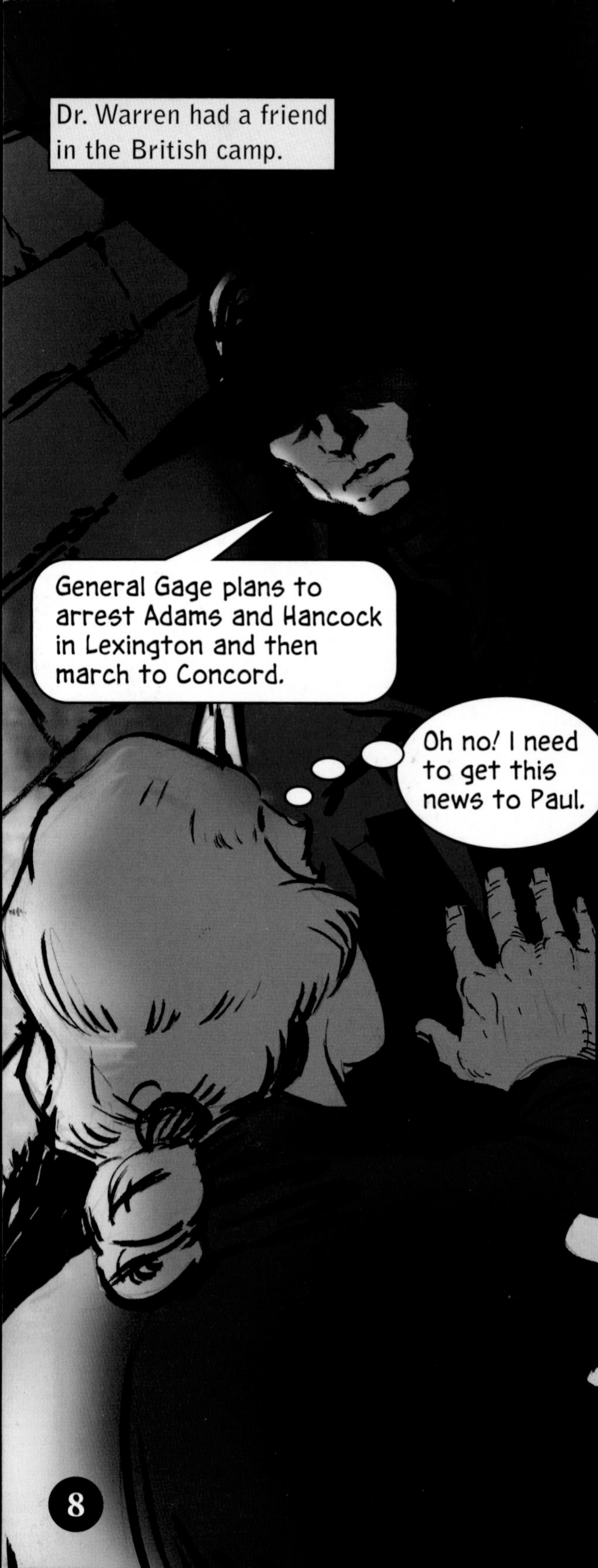
Dr. Warren had a friend in the British camp.
General Gage plans to arrest Adams and Hancock in Lexington and then march to Concord.
Oh no! I need to get this news to Paul.

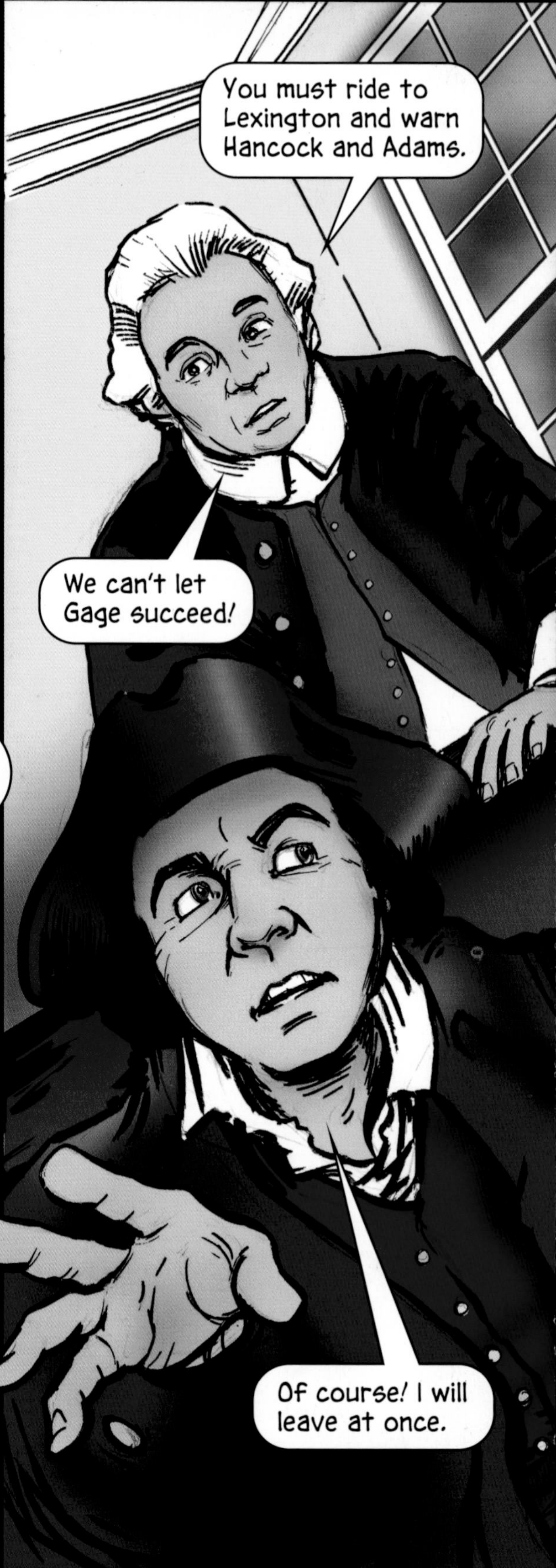
You must ride to Lexington and warn Hancock and Adams.
We can't let Gage succeed!
Of course! I will leave at once.

Revere raced to the house of his friend Robert Newman.
Paul, what's wrong?
General Gage and his troops are moving out by sea! We must warn the others.
Then I'd better get to the North Church.
The two friends had developed a signal to warn Whigs outside Boston. If British troops left the city on foot, Newman would light one lantern in the church tower. If they left by boat, he would light two lanterns.

Chapter 2

The Race to Lexington

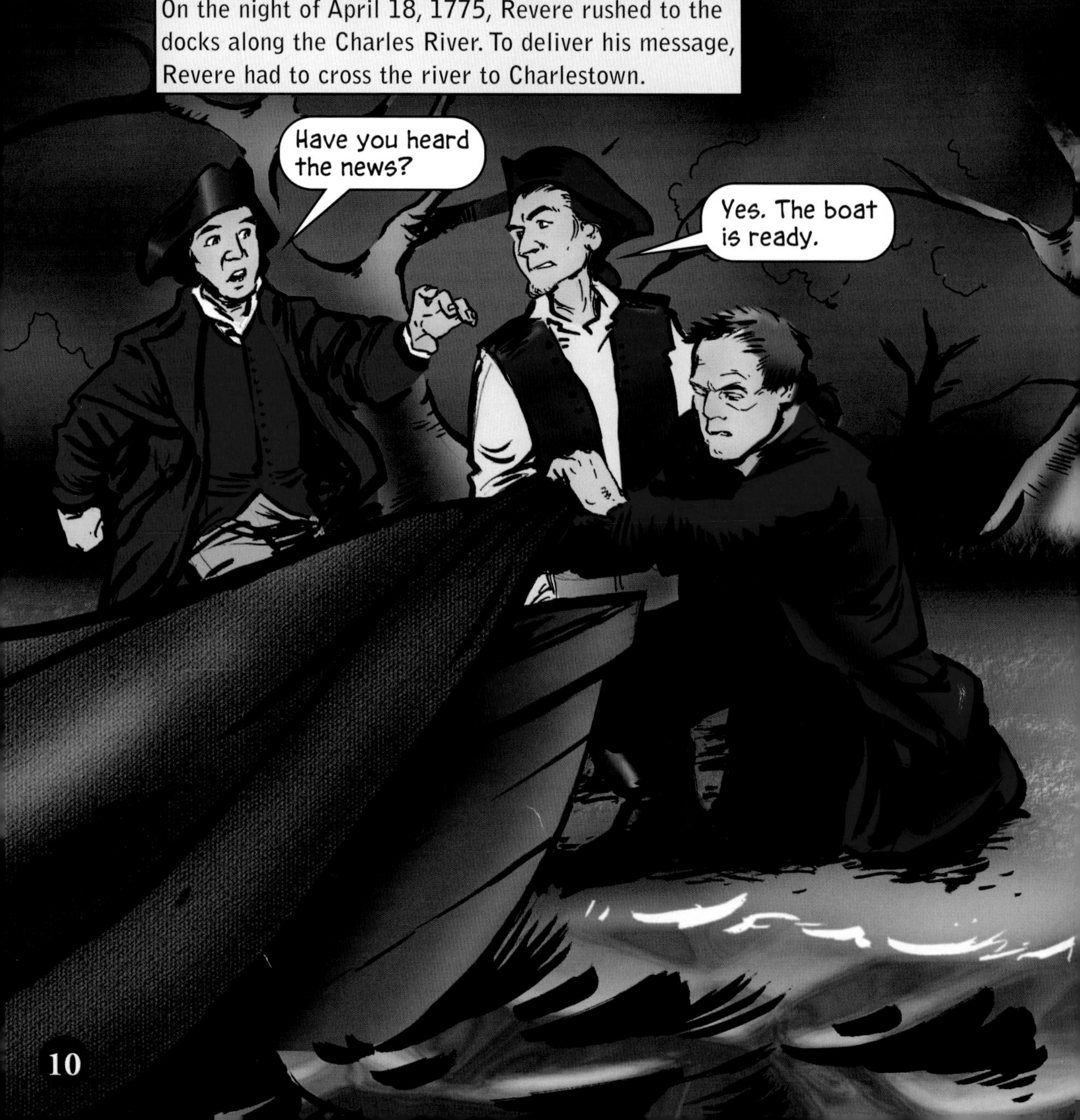
On the night of April 18, 1775, Revere rushed to the docks along the Charles River. To deliver his message, Revere had to cross the river to Charlestown.
Have you heard the news?
Yes. The boat is ready.

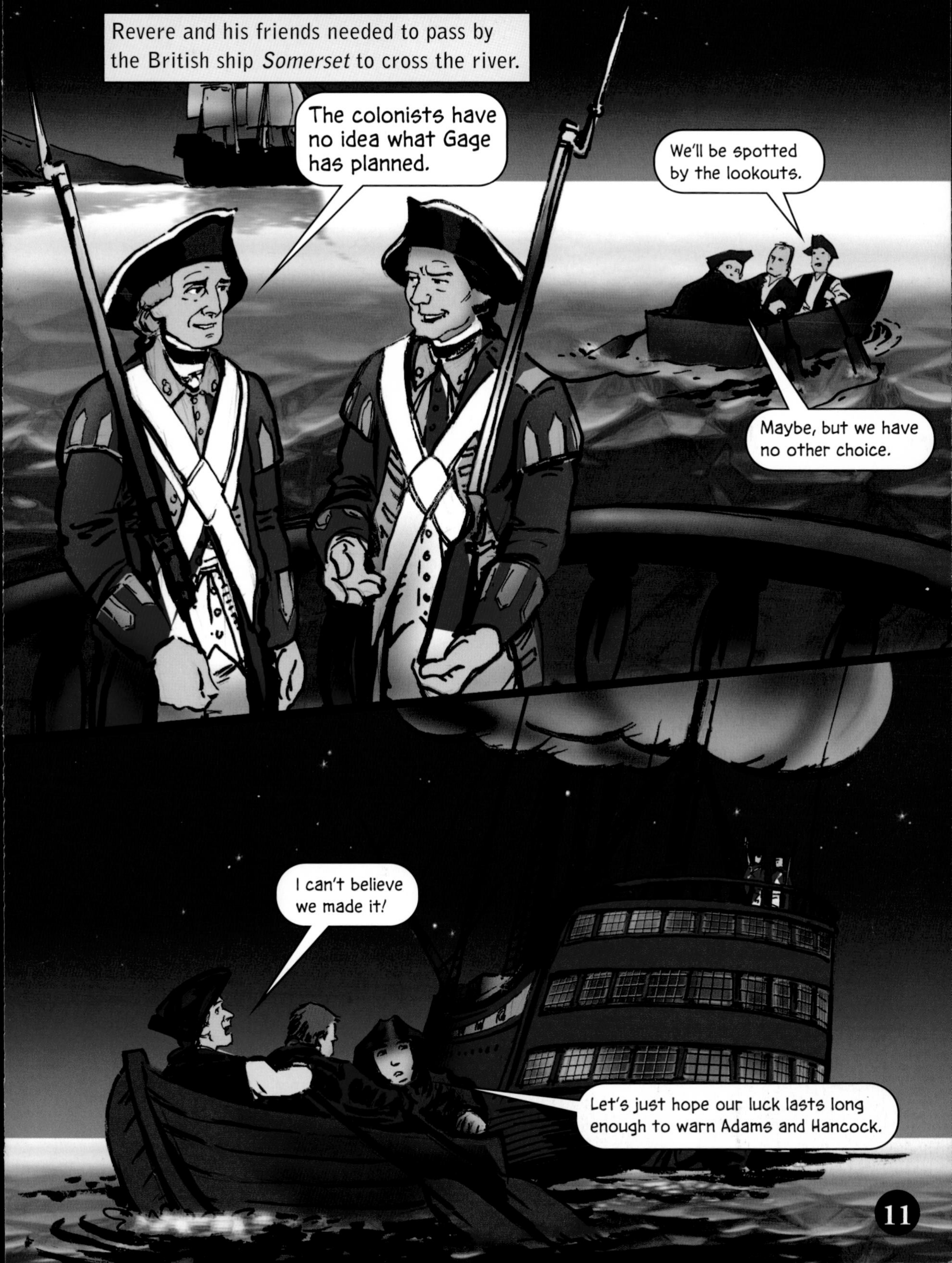
Revere and his friends needed to pass by the British ship *Somerset* to cross the river.
The colonists have no idea what Gage has planned.
We'll be spotted by the lookouts.
Maybe, but we have no other choice.
I can't believe we made it!
Let's just hope our luck lasts long enough to warn Adams and Hancock.

Once in Charlestown, Revere was greeted by Colonel Conant and Richard Devens.

Paul, we received the signal.

Good. I'll borrow a horse from John Larkin and head to Lexington.

I must warn you. There are nine officers, mounted on good horses, and armed, going towards Concord.

Revere ignored the warnings and set off for Lexington. It wasn't long before he ran into trouble.

Stop!

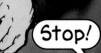

That was too close. I'll need to take a different route.

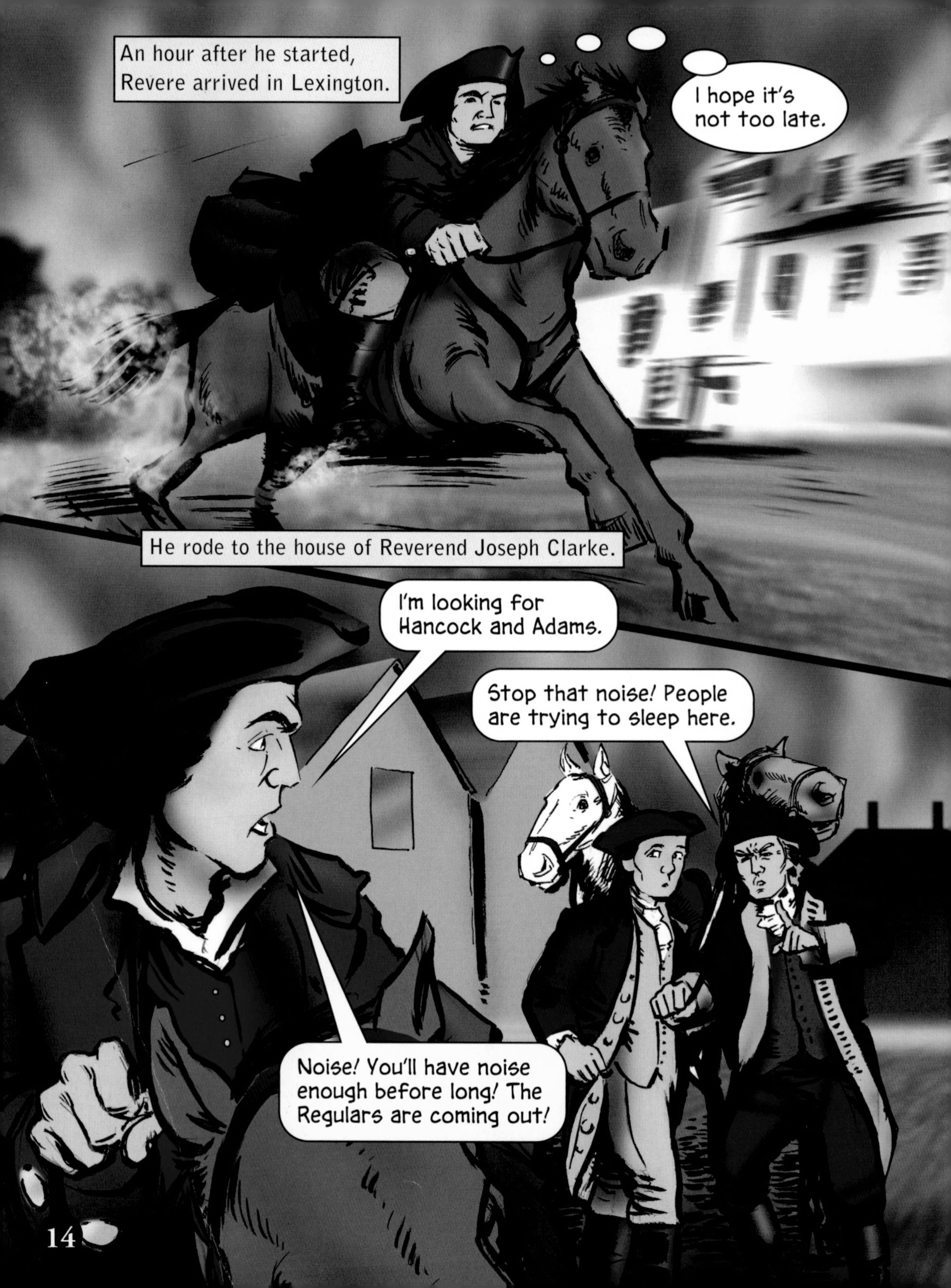
An hour after he started, Revere arrived in Lexington.
I hope it's not too late.
He rode to the house of Reverend Joseph Clarke.
I'm looking for Hancock and Adams.
Stop that noise! People are trying to sleep here.
Noise! You'll have noise enough before long! The Regulars are coming out!

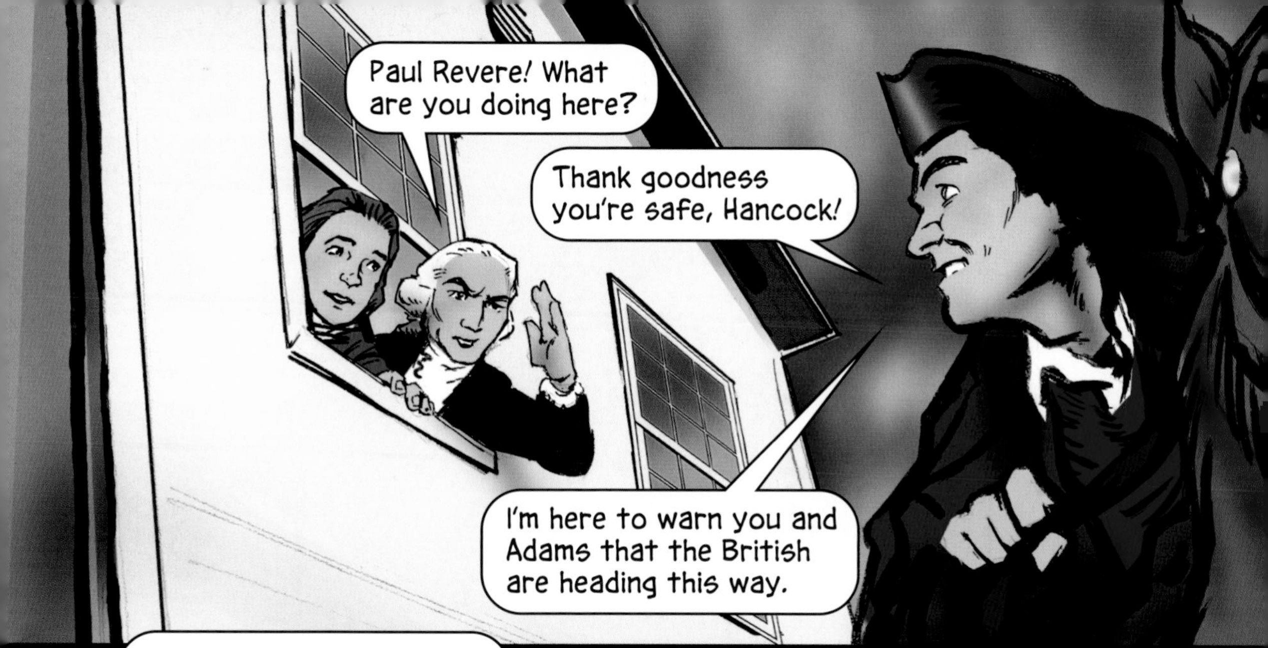
Paul Revere! What are you doing here?
Thank goodness you're safe, Hancock!
I'm here to warn you and Adams that the British are heading this way.

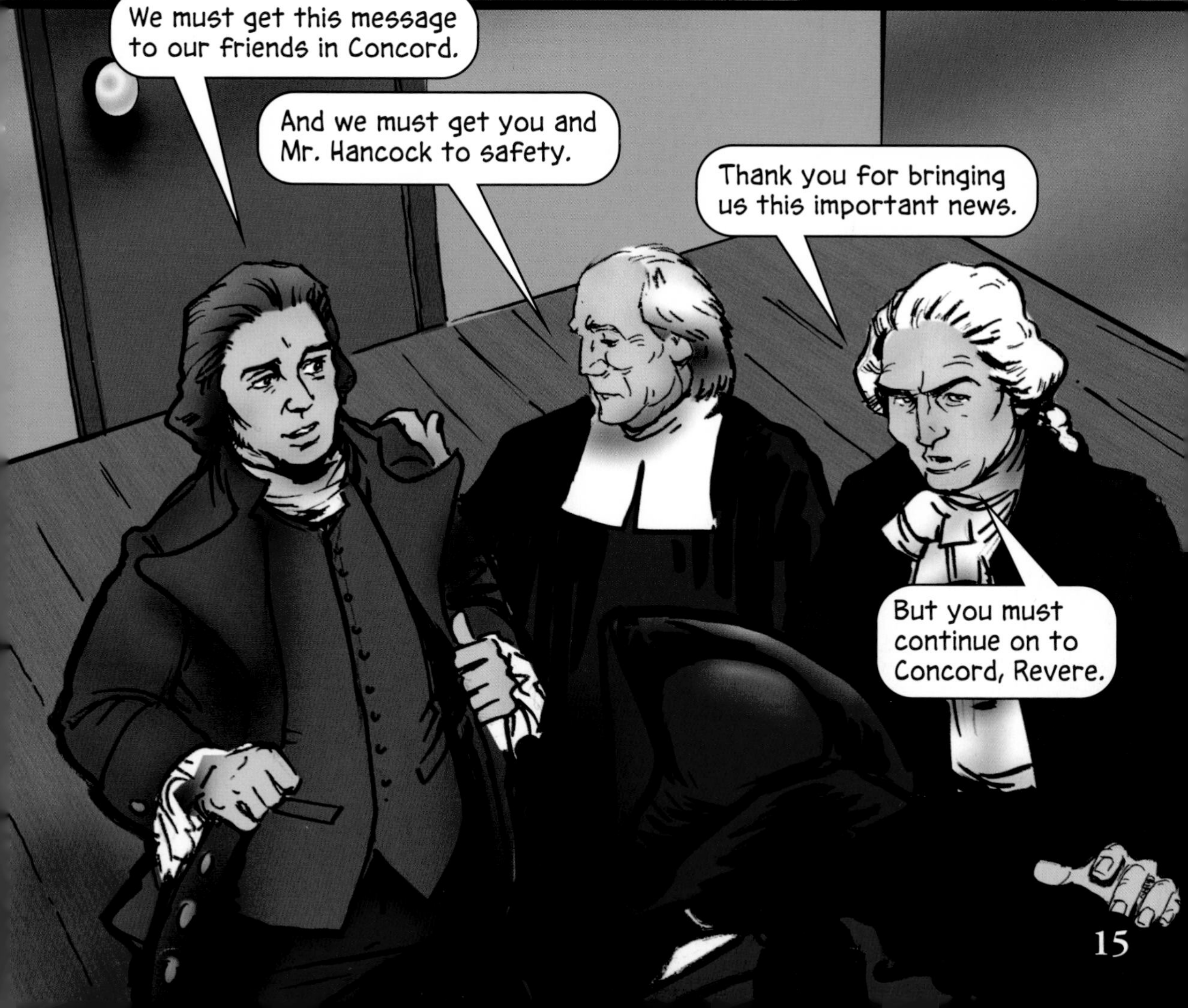
We must get this message to our friends in Concord.
And we must get you and Mr. Hancock to safety.
Thank you for bringing us this important news.
But you must continue on to Concord, Revere.

As the men discussed the next step, another rider from Boston entered.
William Dawes?! I didn't expect to see you here!
Dr. Warren sent me by another route in case you were captured.
After a short rest, Revere and Dawes set out to warn people in Concord.
William, do you hear that?
The church bells are ringing!
It's the signal for the local militia to gather.

As Dawes and Revere headed toward Concord, another rider joined them on the road.
Who goes there?
Dr. Samuel Prescott. What's going on?
The Redcoats are on the march. They are headed to Concord to capture the militia's weapons.
Let me offer my services. Three riders have a better chance of reaching Concord than two.
Revere and Dawes agreed. Together, they continued toward Concord.

Chapter 3

On to Concord

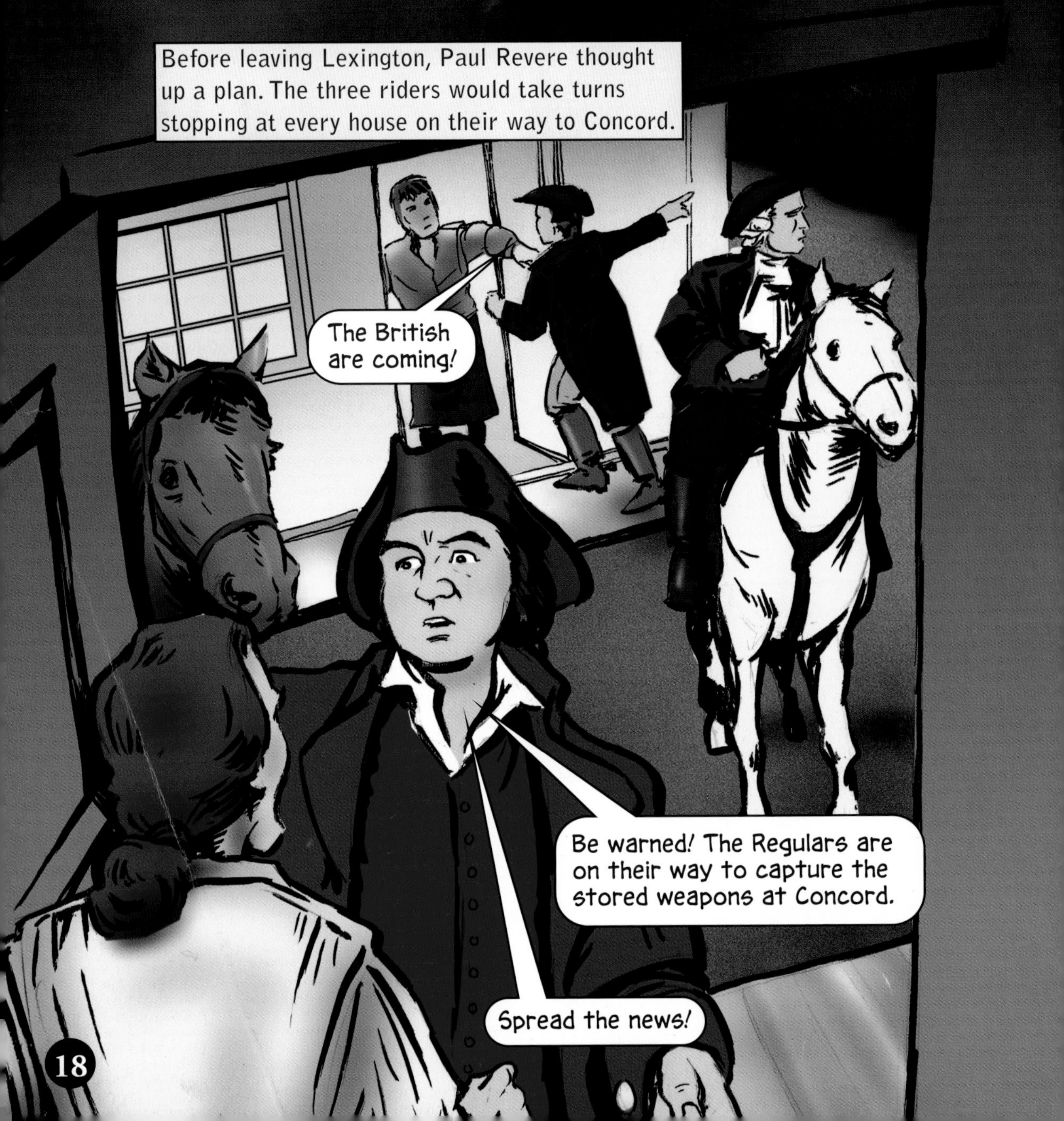

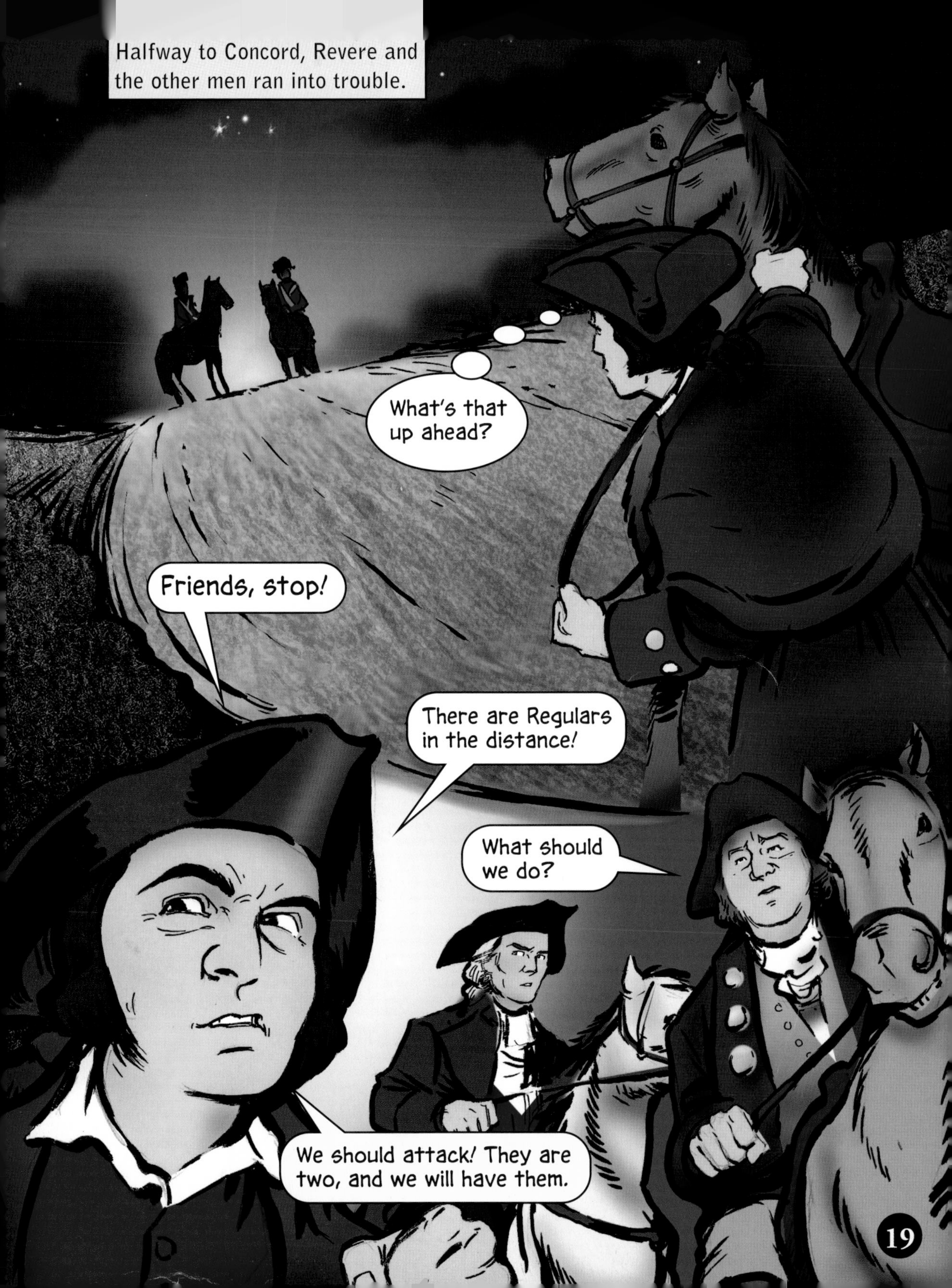
Halfway to Concord, Revere and the other men ran into trouble.
What's that up ahead?
Friends, stop!
There are Regulars in the distance!
What should we do?
We should attack! They are two, and we will have them.

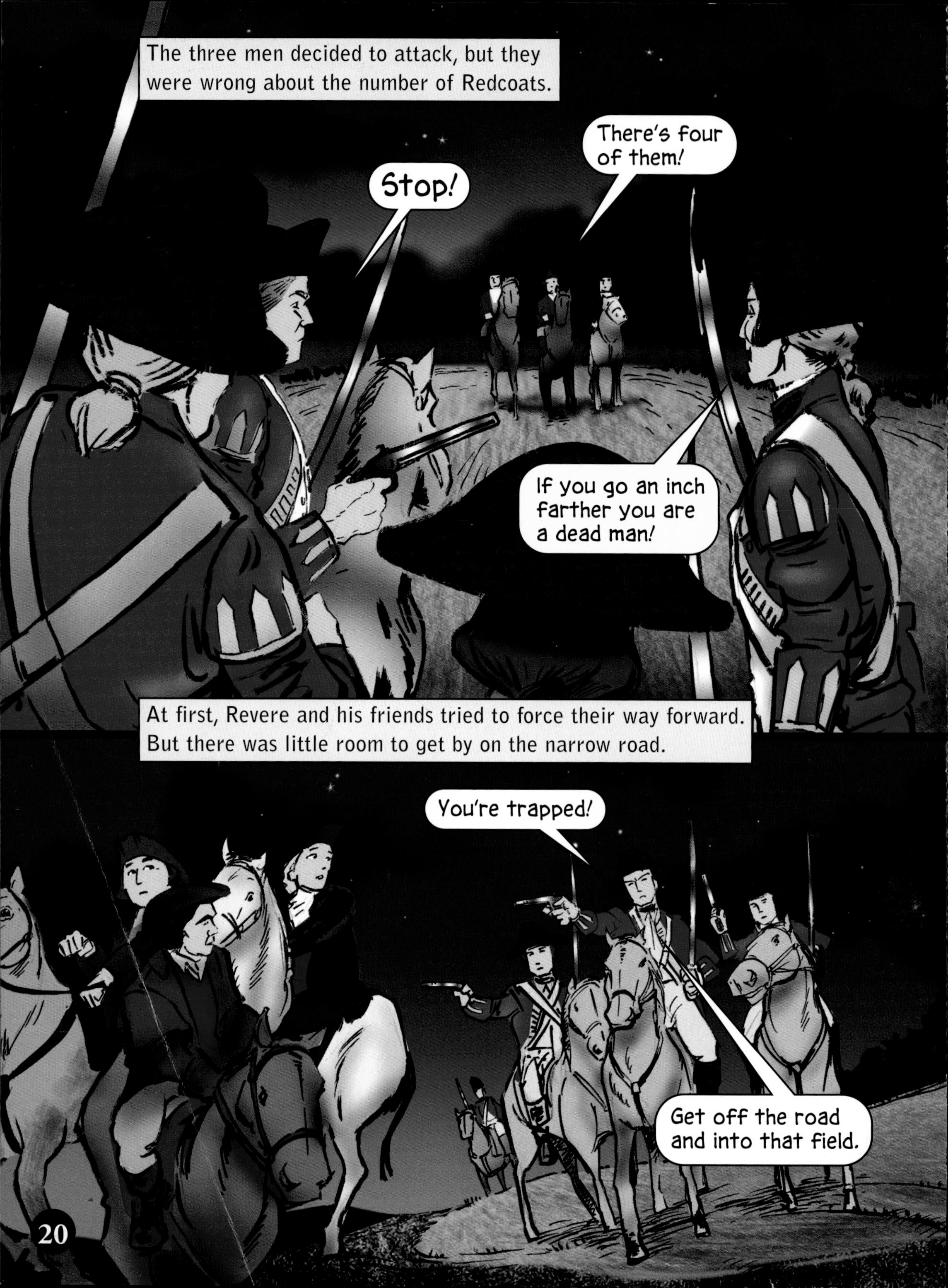
The three men decided to attack, but they were wrong about the number of Redcoats.
Stop!
There's four of them!
If you go an inch farther you are a dead man!
At first, Revere and his friends tried to force their way forward. But there was little room to get by on the narrow road.
You're trapped!
Get off the road and into that field.

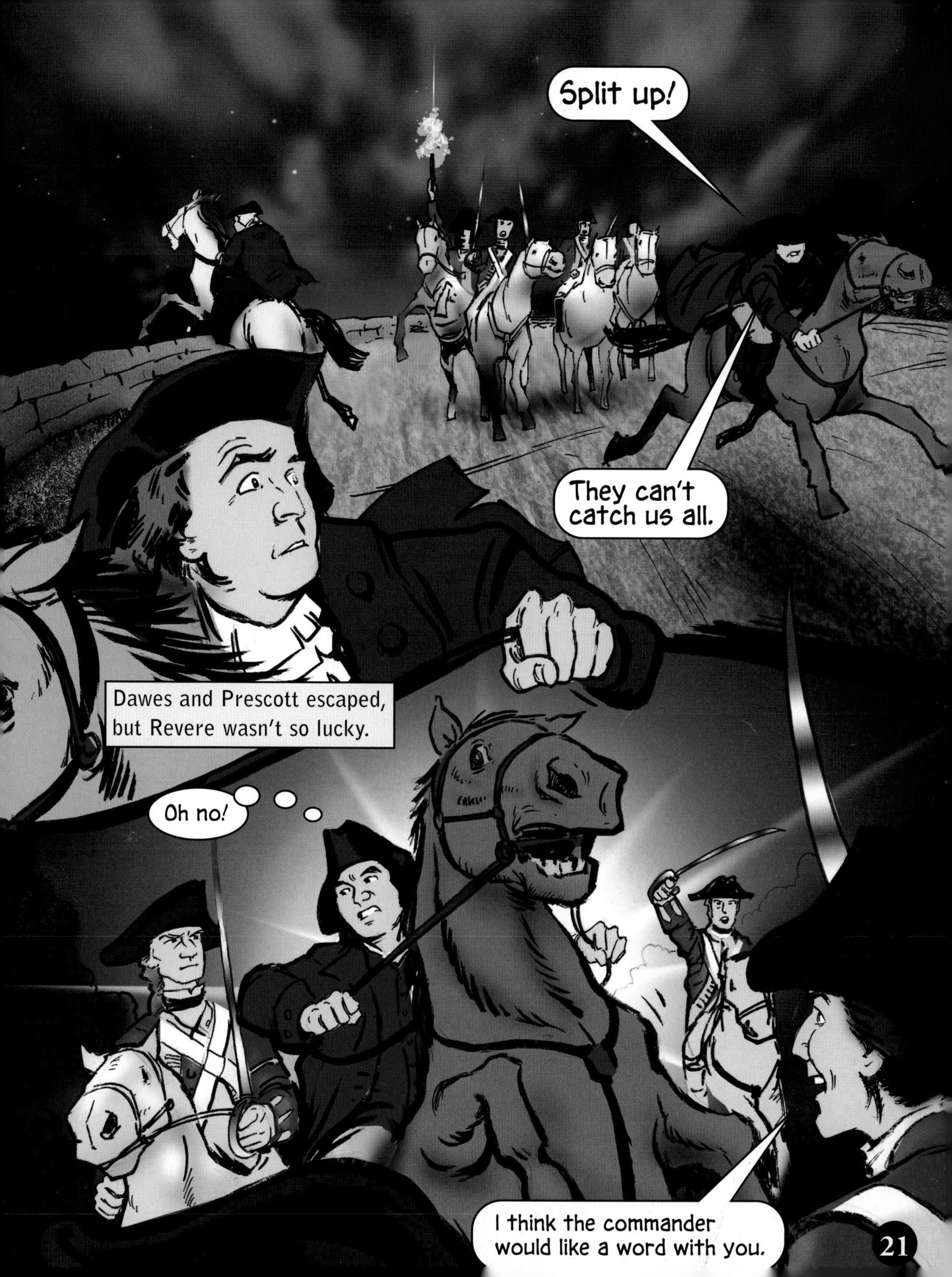
Split up!
They can't catch us all.
Dawes and Prescott escaped, but Revere wasn't so lucky.
Oh no!
I think the commander would like a word with you.

The British decided to check out Revere's story and headed to Lexington. A half mile away from the town, the soldiers heard gunshots.

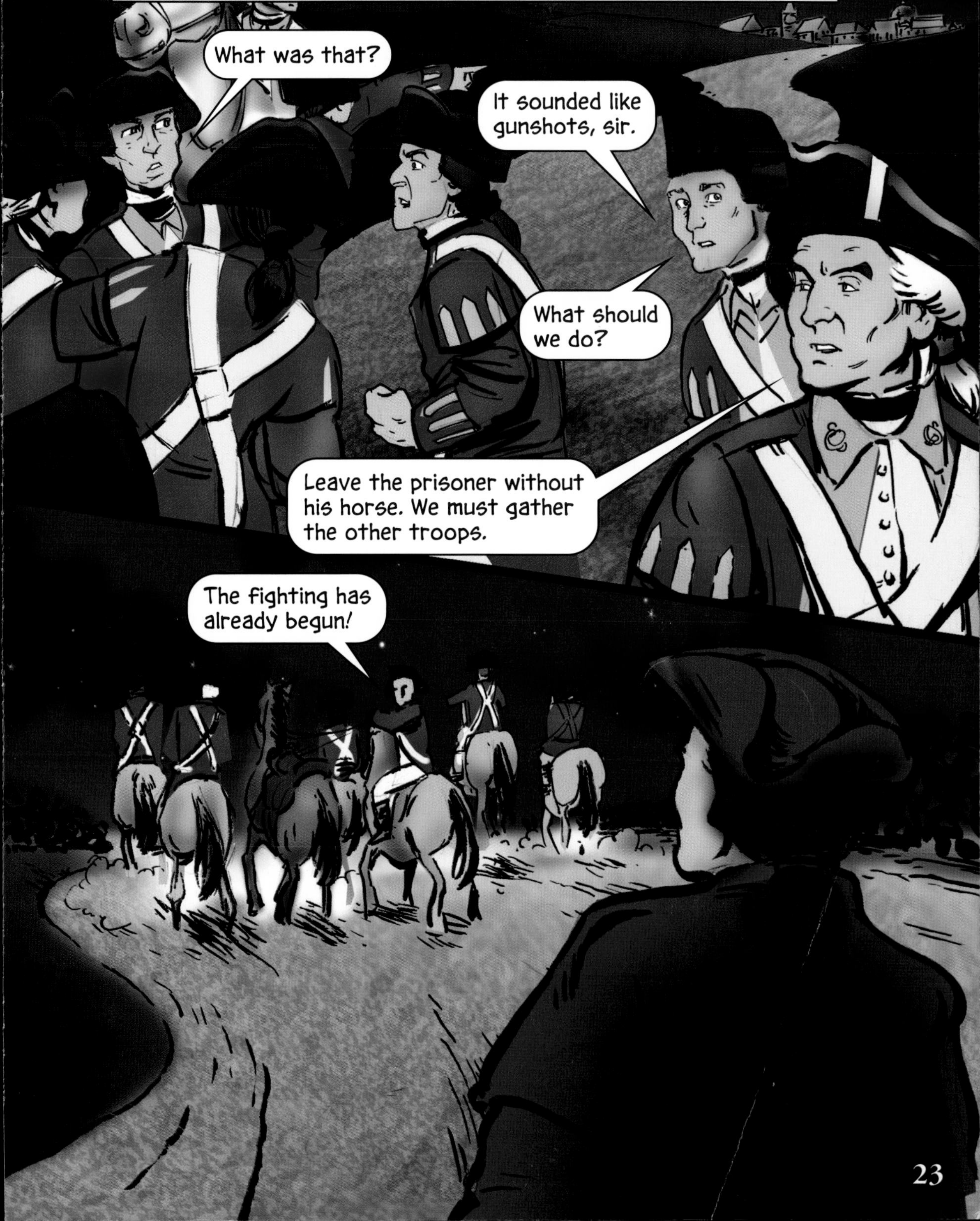
What was that?
It sounded like gunshots, sir.
What should we do?
Leave the prisoner without his horse. We must gather the other troops.
The fighting has already begun!

Chapter 4

The START of a REVOLUTION

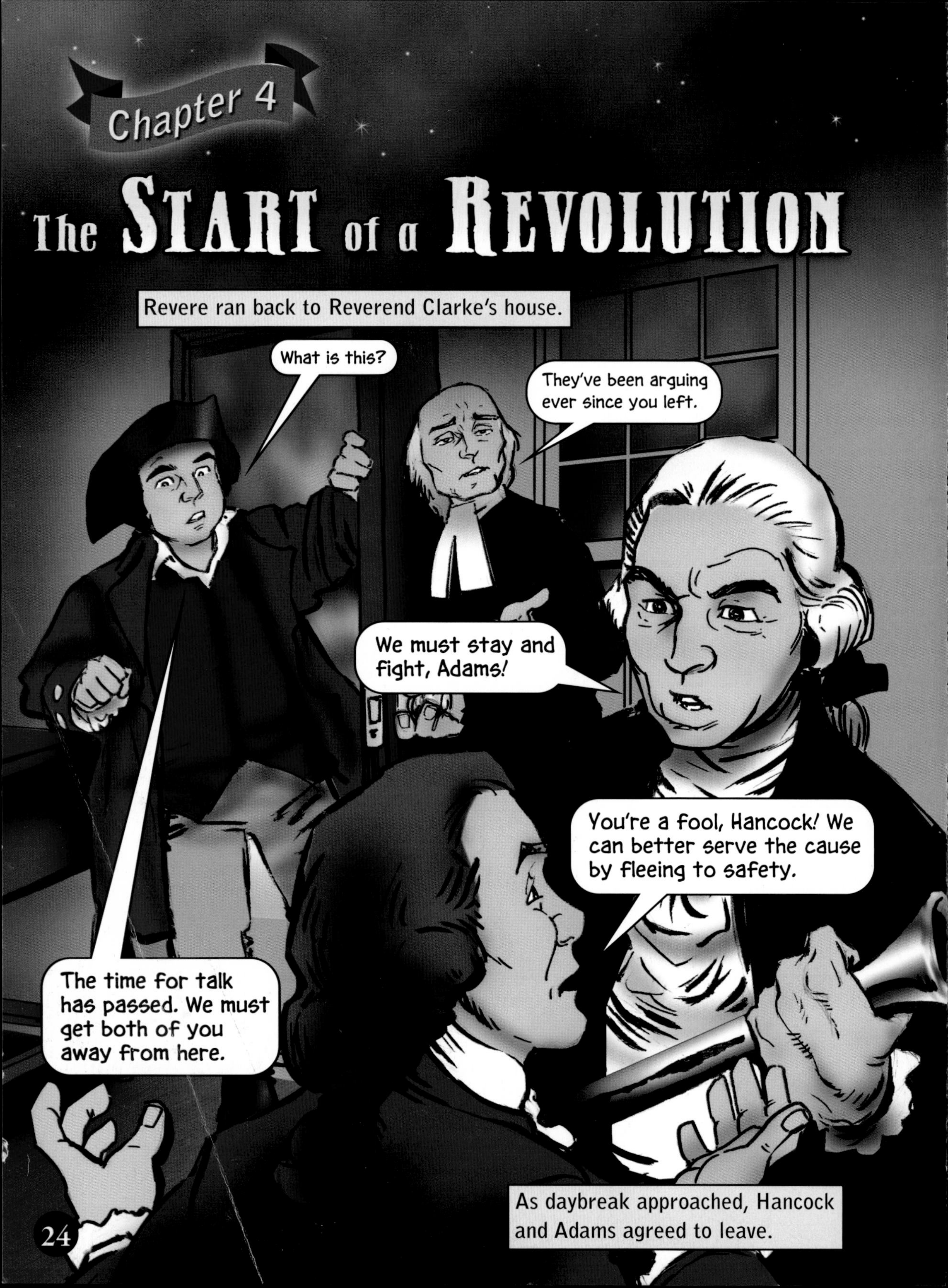

Revere ran back to Reverend Clarke's house.

What is this?

They've been arguing ever since you left.

We must stay and fight, Adams!

You're a fool, Hancock! We can better serve the cause by fleeing to safety.

The time for talk has passed. We must get both of you away from here.

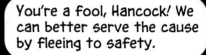

As daybreak approached, Hancock and Adams agreed to leave.

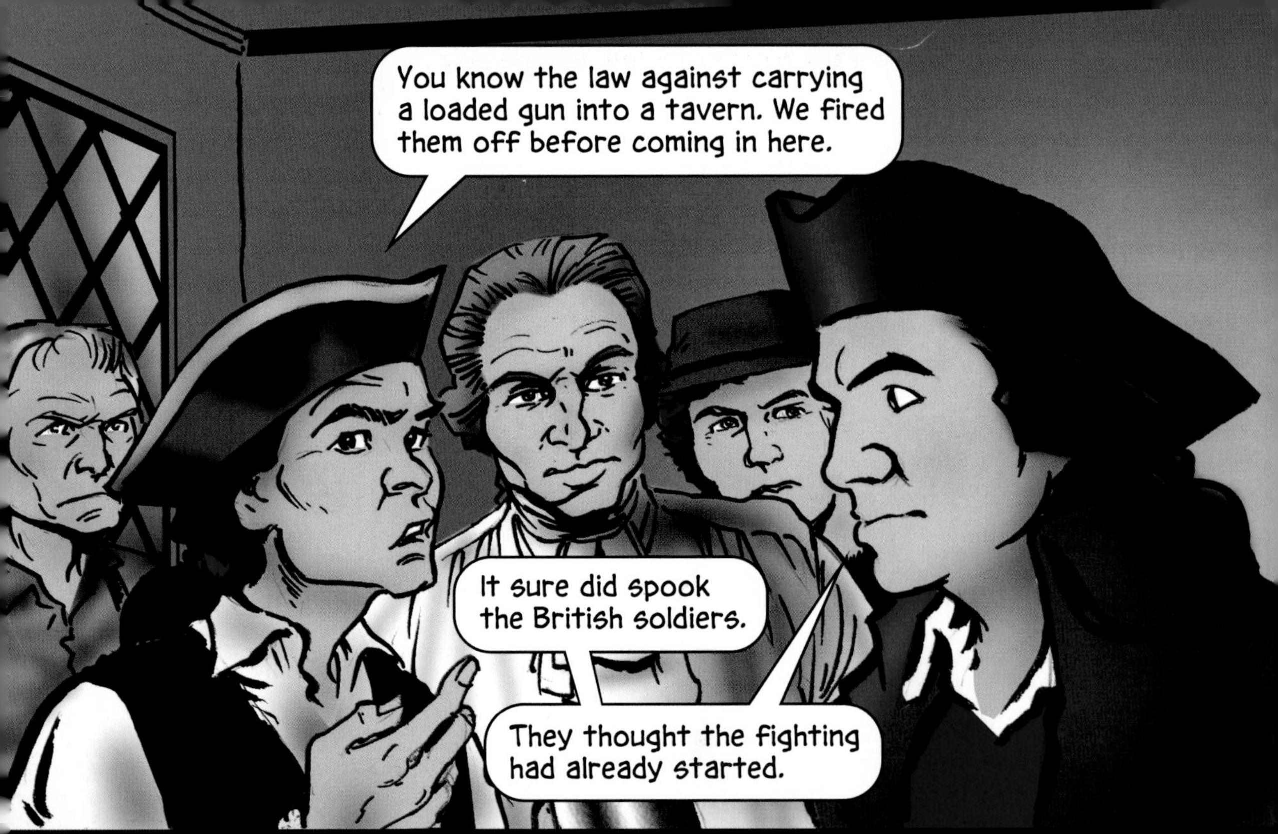
You know the law against carrying a loaded gun into a tavern. We fired them off before coming in here.
It sure did spook the British soldiers.
They thought the fighting had already started.

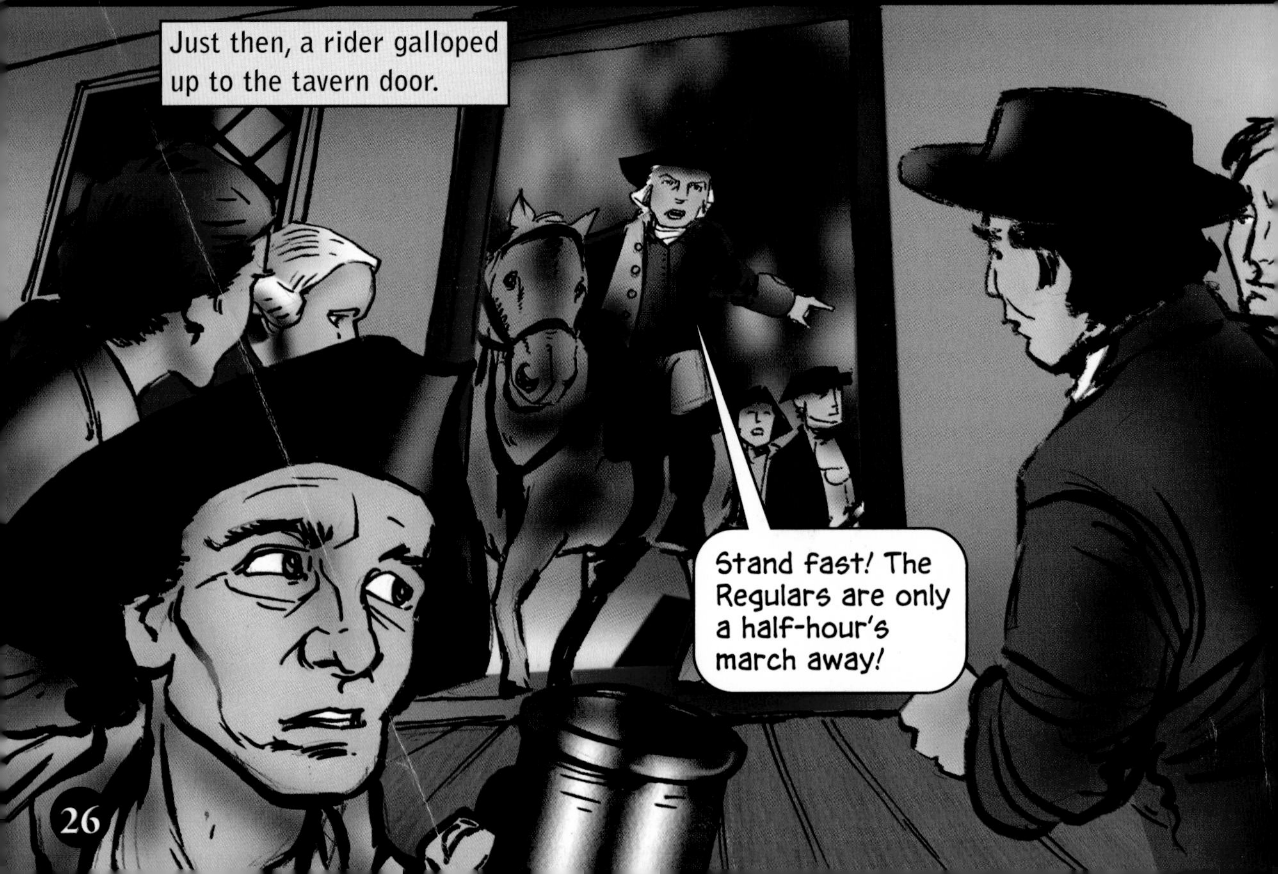
Just then, a rider galloped up to the tavern door.
Stand fast! The Regulars are only a half-hour's march away!

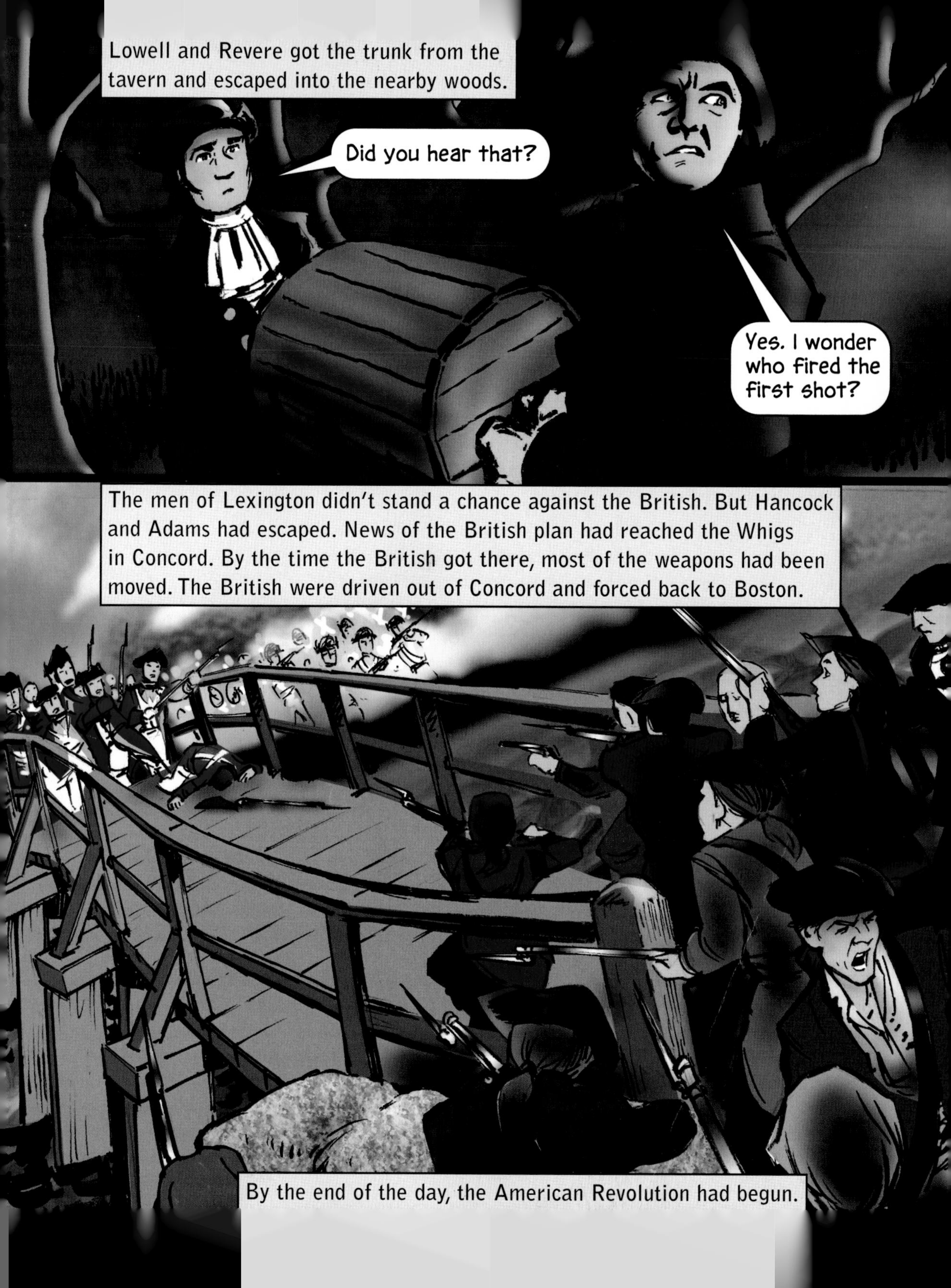
Lowell and Revere got the trunk from the tavern and escaped into the nearby woods.
Did you hear that?
Yes. I wonder who fired the first shot?
The men of Lexington didn't stand a chance against the British. But Hancock and Adams had escaped. News of the British plan had reached the Whigs in Concord. By the time the British got there, most of the weapons had been moved. The British were driven out of Concord and forced back to Boston.
By the end of the day, the American Revolution had begun.

More about

PAUL REVERE'S RIDE

- Paul Revere was born in December 1734. His father, Apollos Rivoire, came to America from France. After marrying an American colonist named Deborah Hichborn, Rivoire changed his name to Revere.

- Paul Revere wasn't just a silversmith. He also made things with gold and copper. He even made false teeth and worked as a dentist. Eventually, Revere launched a successful business making copper sheeting.

- Some people believe the horse Paul Revere borrowed from Larkin was named Brown Beauty. After the British took the horse, neither Revere nor Larkin ever saw the horse again.

- Only 70 militiamen were gathered in Lexington when British troops arrived. They fought against 238 British soldiers. When the battle was over, eight members of the colonial militia were dead. Ten more were wounded. Only one British soldier had been hurt.

- To this day, no one knows who fired the first shot at the Battle of Lexington.

About 700 British troops set out from Boston for Concord. By the time they returned to Boston, more than 250 of the soldiers had been wounded or killed.

 Paul Revere died of natural causes on May 10, 1818. He was 83 years old.

 The heroic deeds of Paul Revere were largely forgotten after the Revolutionary War. In 1860, Henry Wadsworth Longfellow wrote the poem "Paul Revere's Midnight Ride." Soon, the poem and the story of Paul Revere became famous.

 Today, people from all over the world visit Paul Revere's house. It is the oldest building in downtown Boston and a reminder of a great American.

Glossary

militia (muh-LISH-uh)—a group of volunteer citizens who are trained to fight battles

Redcoat (RED-koht)—a British soldier during the Revolutionary War; the name came from the bright red coats the soldiers wore.

representative (rep-ri-ZEN-tuh-tiv)—a person elected to serve in a government

silversmith (SIL-vur-smith)—a person who makes items out of silver, such as spoons, jewelry, and teapots

tax (TAKS)—money collected from a country's citizens to help pay for running the government

Internet Sites

FactHound offers a safe, fun way to find Internet sites related to this book. All of the sites on FactHound have been researched by our staff.

Here's how:

1. Visit *www.facthound.com*
2. Type in this special code **0736849653** for age-appropriate sites. Or enter a search word related to this book for a more general search.
3. Click on the **Fetch It** button.

FactHound will fetch the best sites for you!

READ MORE

Burke, Rick. *Paul Revere.* American Lives. Chicago: Heinemann Library, 2003.

Golden, Nancy. *The British Are Coming!: The Midnight Ride of Paul Revere.* Great Moments in American History. New York: Rosen Central Primary Source, 2004.

Raatma, Lucia. *The Battles of Lexington and Concord.* We the People. Minneapolis: Compass Point Books, 2004.

Rosen, Daniel. *Independence Now: The American Revolution, 1763–1783.* Crossroads America. Washington, DC: National Geographic, 2004.

BIBLIOGRAPHY

Fischer, David Hackett. *Paul Revere's Ride.* New York: Oxford University Press, 1994.

Revere, Paul. *Paul Revere's Three Accounts of His Famous Ride.* Boston: Massachusetts Historical Society, 1976.

Triber, Jayne E. *A True Republican: The Life of Paul Revere.* Amherst: University of Massachusetts Press, 1998.

Index